GLOBALIZATION
AND
The Crucible Of
Global Banking

by Patrick M. Wood

Printed in the United States of America

First Printing, 2018

ISBN 978-0-9863739-3-0
Coherent Publishing, LLC
P.O. Box 52247
Mesa, AZ 85208

Additional Information & Updates
www.Technocracy.News

DEDICATION

This book is dedicated to those who seek knowledge about how the world really works.

But they that will be rich fall into temptation and a snare, and into many foolish and hurtful lusts, which drown men in destruction and perdition. For the love of money is the root of all evil: which while some coveted after. 1 Timothy 6:9-10

TABLE OF CONTENTS

PREFACE

The policies of modern globalization emanated from the Trilateral Commission and its elite membershp beginning in 1973. Founded by global banker David Rockefeller and academic Zbigniew Brzezinski, the Commission was the first action-oriented organization dedicated to fostering a "New International Economic Order."

The Commission was differentiated from a mere policy center by the character and nature of its membership and its stated goals. Its membership included multinational corporation executives, banking executives, media leaders, powerful legal firms, leading academics and most importantly, top leaders in government. In 1973, the global economic system was primarily dominated by the United States, Europe and Japan, and Commission membership was generally drawn from these regions on an equal basis.

As concensus of the general membership was hammered out behind closed doors, government members pushed policies from the top down through political action while corporate, media and legal action pushed from the bottom up. In short, this became the crucible of globalization that has transformed the world in unimaginable ways.

For an abundance of documentation on the early days of globalization, the reader should see *Trilaterals Over Washington, Volumes I and II*, which were co-authored by this writer and the late Professor Antony C. Sutton. The later stages of this crucible are revealed in *Technocracy Rising: The Trojan Horse of Global Transformation* and *Technocracy: The Hard Road to World Order*.

The purpose of this book is to shed additional light on the most important *tool* of globalization, namely, Global Banking. It is ever important to "follow the money" when trying to figure out complex geo-political events and trends. In the case of globalization, that would lead us to the three most important banking institutions on the planet: the World Bank, the International Monetary Fund and the Bank for International Settlements. It will be immediately noted that these are not profit-driven commercial banks like Bank of America, Citigroup, Chase Manhattan (now JPMorgan Chase) or Goldman Sachs. Rather, they were supra-national money centers that laundered funds from nation to nation for the purpose of forcing pre-determined political and economic outcomes. Furthermore, it is key to understand how they cooperate and coordinate as a team to achieve their desired ends.

John Perkins, international finance whistle-blower and author of the best-selling book *Confessions of* an *Economic Hit Man* in 2004, wrote:

Economic hit men are highly paid professionals who cheat countries around the globe out of trillions of dollars. They funnel money from the World Bank, the U.S. Agency for International Development, and other foreign "aid" organizations into the coffers of huge corporations and the pockets of a few wealthy families who control the planet's natural resources. Their tools include fraudulent financial reports, rigged elections, payoffs, extortion, sex, and murder. They play a game as old as empire, but one that has taken on new and terrifying dimensions during this time of globalization. I should know; I was an economic hit man.[1]

Regardless of Perkins' motives or political persuasion in writing this expose, it does reveal elements of the dark underbelly of global finance. It is nothing short of the plundering the planet for money and natural resources.

With this in mind, *Globalization in the Crucible of Global Banking* offers a broad understanding of global finance and how it has been used to drive nations into the Trilateral Commission's New International Economic Order.

Except for a few minor edits, the text remains the same as when this writer sketched out these topics from 2005 through 2007. Nothing has changed since then, except for the introduction of crypto-currencies; the reader can rest assured that the global banking cartel is hard at work to maintain its total dominance.

---

1 Perkins, John, 1945-. Confessions Of an Economic Hit Man. San Francisco, CA :Berrett-Koehler, 2004, Preface.

CHAPTER 1

THE INTERNATIONAL MONETARY FUND

The International Monetary Fund (IMF) is:
a public institution, established with money provided by taxpayers around the world. This is important to remember because it does not report directly to either the citizens who finance it or those whose lives it affects. Rather, it reports to the ministries of finance and the central banks of the governments of the world.[1]

This authoritative statement comes from Joseph Stiglitz, who served for seven years as chairman of President Clinton's Council of Economic Advisers and as chief economist for the World Bank. Stiglitz is a mainstream globalist, but still honest enough to have become disillusioned with the corrupt practices of the IMF and the World Bank. His first-hand witness is very insightful:

International bureaucrats - the faceless symbols of the world economic order - are under attack everywhere. Formerly uneventful meetings of obscure technocrats discussing mundane subjects such as concessional loans and trade quotas have now become the scene of raging street battles and huge demonstrations... Virtually every major meeting of the International Monetary Fund, the World Bank, and the World Trade Organization is now the scene of conflict and turmoil.[2]

Why is the IMF an organization that people love to hate? This report will shed some light on the subject.

---

1   Stiglitz, Globalization and its Discontents (Norton, 2002), p.12
2   ibid, p. 3

IMF Beginnings

According to its own literature, the IMF was "established to promote international monetary cooperation, exchange stability, and orderly exchange arrangements; to foster economic growth and high levels of employment; and to provide temporary financial assistance to countries to help ease balance of payments adjustment."

This innocuous description hardly describes the critical functions that the IMF provides to the process of globalization. Indeed, the IMF is one of the leading agents of change in the global economy and global governance.

The IMF was actually created in December, 1945 when the first 29 member nations signed its Articles of Agreement, and began operations on March 1, 1947. (Note: there are 184 member countries today.)

The authorization for the IMF came a few months earlier at the famous Bretton Woods conference of July 1944.

On the heels of World War II, the Bretton Woods Agreements established a system of procedures and rules, together with institutions to enforce them, that called for member countries to adopt a monetary policy that was fixed in terms of gold. Although the Bretton Woods system utterly collapsed in 1971 after President Nixon suspended convertibility of the dollar into gold, the institutions created in 1944 continued on uninterrupted.

While any country may become a member of the IMF, the road to membership is noteworthy. When application for membership is submitted to the IMF's executive board, a "Membership Resolution" is made to the Board of Governors that covers the member's quota, subscription and voting rights. If approved by the Board of Governors, the applicant must amend its own laws in order to permit it to sign the IMF's Articles of Agreement and to otherwise fulfill the obligations required of members. In other words, the member subordinates a certain part of its legal sovereignty to the IMF. This sets the stage for the IMF to take an active role in the affairs of the member country.

The IMF is viewed by some as a global organization, but it should be noted that the U.S. has 18.25 percent of the vote on the

IMF board, or three times more than any other member. In addition, the IMF is based in Washington, DC.

IMF Founders: Harry Dexter White and John Maynard Keynes

The principal architects of the Bretton Woods system, and hence the IMF, were Harry Dexter White and John Maynard Keynes.

Keynes was an English economist who has had an enormous impact on global economic thinking despite the fact that many of his economic theories have been thoroughly discredited. During WWII, he had called for the dissolution of the Bank for International Settlements because of its domination by Nazi operatives. After WWII however, when disbanding the BIS was actually mandated by Congress, he argued against the dissolution pending the creation of the IMF and World Bank. His latter argument was the often and over-used rationale "If we close it down too soon, the world financial system will collapse." Keynes globalist instincts led him to call for a world currency, called Bancor, that would be managed by a global central bank. This idea flatly failed.

Harry Dexter White was also considered to be a brilliant economist, and was appointed in as 1942 assistant to Henry Morgenthau, Secretary of the Treasury. He remained Morgenthau's most trusted assistant throughout his term, and argued verbosely against the Bank for International Settlements. Like Morgenthau and most all Americans, White was strongly anti-Nazi. White, however, was NOT pro-American.[3]

On October 16, 1950, an FBI memo identified White as a Soviet spy whose code name was Jurist.

Following the collapse of the Soviet Union in 1991, formerly secret intelligence documents were made public and shined new light on the matter. White was not just a spy among the 50-odd identified American spies, he was likely the top spy for the USSR in the U.S.

In 1999, the Hoover Digest wrote:

---

3   Ladd, FBI Office Memorandum, October 16, 1950

*In their new book Venona: Decoding Soviet Espionage in
America, Harvey Klehr and John Haynes argue that of some
fifty Americans known to have spied for Stalin (many more
have never been identified), Harry Dexter White was prob-
ably the most important agent.[4]*

Had White lived beyond 1946, he likely would have been pros-
ecuted for high treason against the U.S., the penalty for which is
execution.

Such is the moral fiber and intellectual credentials of the creators of the IMF: One was a English ideologue economist with a
markedly global bent, and the other a corrupt and high-ranking
U.S. government official who was a top Soviet spy.

Trying to figure out where these two really stood in the eyes
of the core global elite has more twists than a Sherlock Holmes
mystery story. It is more easily perceived by the end result -- the
successful creation of the IMF and the World Bank, both of which
were heartily endorsed by the likes of J.P. Morgan and Chase Bank
(now JPMorganChase), among other international bankers.

Positioning: IMF vs. the World Bank and the BIS

There is a triad of monetary powers that rule global money operations: the IMF, the World Bank and the Bank for International
Settlements. Although they work together very closely, it is necessary to see which part each plays in the globalization process.

The International Monetary Fund (IMF) and the World Bank
interact only with governments whereas the BIS interacts only
with other central banks. The IMF loans money to national governments, and often these countries are in some kind of fiscal or
monetary crisis. Furthermore, the IMF raises money by receiving "quota" contributions from its 184 member countries. Even
though the member countries may borrow money to make their
quota contributions, it is, in reality, all tax-payer money.[5]

The World Bank also lends money to governments and has 184
member countries. Within the World Bank are two separate entities, the International Bank for Reconstruction and Development
(IBRD) and the International Development Association (IDA).

---

4   Beichman, Guilty as Charged, Hoover Digest 1999 No. 2
5   IMF web site, http://www.imf.org

The IBRD focuses on middle income and credit-worthy poor countries, while the IDA focuses on the poorest of nations. The World Bank is self-sufficient for internal operations, borrowing money by direct lending from banks and by floating bond issues, and then loaning this money through IBRD and IDA to troubled countries.[6]

The BIS, as central bank to the other central banks, facilitates the movement of money. They are well-known for issuing "bridge loans" to central banks in countries where IMF or World Bank money is pledged but has not yet been delivered. These bridge loans are then repaid by the respective governments when they receive the funds that had been promised by the IMF or World Bank.[7]

The IMF has become known as the "lender of last resort." When a country starts to crumble because of problems with trade deficits or excessive debt burdens, the IMF can step in and bail it out. If the country were a patient in a hospital, the treatment would include a transfusion and other life support measures to just keep the patient alive -- full recovery is not really in view, nor has it ever happened.

One must remember that rescue operations would not be necessary if it were not for the central banks, international banks, the IMF and the World Bank leading these countries into debts they cannot possibly ever repay in the first place.

The Purpose and Structure of the IMF

According to the IMF pamphlet, *A Global Institution: The IMF's Role at a Glance,*

The IMF is the central institution of the international monetary system—the system of international payments and exchange rates among national currencies that enables business to take place between countries.

It aims to prevent crises in the system by encouraging countries to adopt sound economic policies; it is also—as its name suggests—a fund that can be tapped by members needing

---

6   World Bank web site. http://www.WorldBank.org
7   Baker, The Bank for International Settlements: Evolution and Evaluation, (Quorum, 2002), p. 141-142

temporary financing to address balance of payments problems.

- *The IMF works for global prosperity by promoting*
- *the balanced expansion of world trade,*
- *stability of exchange rates,*
- *avoidance of competitive devaluations, and*
- *orderly correction of balance of payments problems.*

The IMF's statutory purposes include promoting the balanced expansion of world trade, the stability of exchange rates, the avoidance of competitive currency devaluations, and the orderly correction of a country's balance of payments problems.[8]

Although the IMF has changed in significant ways over the years, their current literature makes it quite clear that the statutory purposes of the IMF today are the same as when they were formulated in 1944:

i. To promote international monetary cooperation through a permanent institution which provides the machinery for consultation and collaboration on international monetary problems.

ii. To facilitate the expansion and balanced growth of international trade, and to contribute thereby to the promotion and maintenance of high levels of employment and real income and to the development of the productive resources of all members as primary objectives of economic policy.

iii. To promote exchange stability, to maintain orderly exchange arrangements among members, and to avoid competitive exchange depreciation.

iv. To assist in the establishment of a multilateral system of payments in respect of current transactions between members and in the elimination of foreign exchange restrictions which hamper the growth of world trade.

v. To give confidence to members by making the general resources of the Fund temporarily available to them under ad-

---

8   IMF, What is the International Monetary Fund?, 2004

equate safeguards, thus providing them with opportunity to correct maladjustments in their balance of payments without resorting to measures destructive of national or international prosperity.

vi. In accordance with the above, to shorten the duration and lessen the degree of disequilibrium in the international balances of payments of members.[9]

As lofty as this might sound, one can interpret meanings by matching up its actions. For instance, "consultation and collaboration" often means "we will enforce our policies on your country" and "adequate safeguards" mean the "collateral and concessions we demand in return for borrowing our money."

The IMF has been likened to an international credit union, where members who contribute reserves have the opportunity to borrow as the need may arise. The IMF is further able to raise funds by borrowing from member countries or from private markets. The IMF claims to have not raised funds from private markets as of yet.

This chapter will examine four aspects of IMF operations: Currency and monetary roles, moral hazard, bailout operations during currency crisis and conditionalities.

Currency, Monetary Roles and Gold

Two years prior to the collapse of the Bretton Woods system, the IMF created a reserve mechanism called the Special Drawing Right, or SDR.

The SDR is not a currency, nor is it a liability of the IMF, rather it is primarily a potential claim on freely usable currencies. Freely usable currencies, as determined by the IMF, are the U.S. dollar, euro, Japanese yen, and pound sterling.[10]

Since the value of the component currencies change relative to each other, the value of the SDR changes relative to each component. As of December 29, 2005, one SDR was valued at $1.4291. The SDR interest rate was pegged at 3.03 percent.

There should be no mistake in the readers mind that the IMF

9   Ibid.
10   IMF, Overview of the IMF as a Financial Institution, p.11

correctly views itself as the "currency controller" for all countries who have hitched a ride on the globalization express. According to an official publication:

The IMF is therefore concerned not only with the problems of individual countries but also with the working of the international monetary system as a whole. Its activities are aimed at promoting policies and strategies through which its members can work together to ensure a stable world financial system and sustainable economic growth. The IMF provides a forum for international monetary cooperation, and thus for an orderly evolution of the system, and it subjects a wide area of international monetary affairs to the covenants of law, moral suasion, and understandings.[11]

The IMF works closely with the Bank for International Settlements in promoting smooth currency markets, exchange rates, monetary policy, etc. The BIS, as central bank for central banks, more likely tells the IMF what to do rather than vice versa. This notion is bolstered by the fact that on March 10, 2003, the BIS adopted the SDR as its official reserve asset, abandoning the 1930 gold Swiss franc altogether.

This action removed all restraint from the creation of paper money in the world. In other words, gold backs no national currency, leaving the central banks a wide-open field to create money as they alone see fit. Remember, that almost all the central banks in the world are privately- or jointly-held entities, with an exclusive franchise to arrange loans for their respective host countries.

This is not to say that gold has no current or future role in international money. Under Bretton Woods, gold was the central reserve asset, and original subscribers contributed large amounts of gold bullion. Gold was abandoned completely in 1971, but the IMF continues to own and hold gold into the present: 103.4 million ounces (3,217 metric tons) with a current market value of about $45 billion. This is no small amount of gold!

The U.S. Treasury claims to have 261.5 million ounces of gold, but there has never been an official, physical audit of Fort Knox and other repositories to back up this claim. By comparison,

---

11   ibid, p. 3

Great Britain claims to own 228 million ounces of gold.

The BIS, IMF and major central banks (notably the New York Federal Reserve Bank and the Bank of England) have collectively and methodically sold portions of their gold stocks while claiming that "gold is dead". This manipulation has tended to suppress the price of gold since the early 1970's. Antony Sutton's 1979 book, The War on Gold, dealt definitively on this matter. More recently, the group Gold Anti-Trust Action Committee (GATA) was founded in 1999 with essentially the same argument: gold has been unfairly manipulated.

Suffice it to say that if so many organizations have conspired to keep "gold as money" out of the public mind, then gold is not dead but just temporarily on the shelf. When fiat currencies have been drained dry by the global cartel, gold will likely be brought back by the same people who told us it was forever a dead issue.

Moral Hazard

This is a technical legal term with a precise meaning, but it is easily understood. Moral hazard is the term given to the increased risk of immoral behavior resulting in a negative outcome (the "hazard"), because the persons who increased the risk potential in the first place either suffer no consequences, or benefit from it.

While the IMF is riddled with specific instances of moral hazard, its very existence is a moral hazard.

The eminent economist Hans F. Sennholz (Grove City College) sums up the IMF operations this way:

The IMF actually encourages bankers and investors to take imprudent risk by providing taxpayer funds to bail them out. It encourages corrupt governments to engage in boom and bust policies by coming to their rescue whenever they run out of dollar reserves.[12]

The money shuffle goes like this: The World Bank and the BIS develop markets for credit by enticing governments to borrow money. They (and the private banks along side of them) are encouraged to make risky loans because they know that IMF stands ready to rescue countries with defaulting loans -- the moral haz-

12   Sennholz, IMF Bailouts Make Matters Worse

ard. As the usury interest builds up and finally threatens the entire financial stability of the affected country, the IMF steps in with
a "bail out" operation. Defaulted loans are replaced or restruc-
tured with (taxpayer provided) IMF loans. Additional money is
loaned to repay back interest and allow for further expansion of
the economy. In the end, the desperate country is even further in
debt and is now saddled with all kinds of additional restrictions
and conditions. Plus, under the phony aegis of "poverty reduction", citizens are invariably left worse off than in the beginning.

Conditionalities

This is also a technical term that has a specific meaning: A conditionality is a condition attached to a loan or a debt relief granted by the IMF or the World Bank. Conditionalities are typically
non-financial in nature, such as requiring a country to privatize
or deregulate key public services.

Conditionalities are most significant within so-called Structural
Adjustment Programs (SAP) created by the IMF. Nations are required to implement or promise to implement the attached conditionalities prior to approval of the loan.

The fallout of conditionalities is notable. The globalist think-
tank Foreign Policy in Focus published *IMF Bailouts and Global
Financial Flows* by Dr. David Felix in 1998. The report's introduction makes these key points:

1. *The IMF has been transformed into an instrument for
    prying open third world markets to foreign capital and
    for collecting foreign debts.*

2. *This transformation violates the IMF charter in spirit
    and substance, and has increased the costs to countries
    requesting IMF financial aid.*

3. *The IMF's operational crisis stems from growing debtor
    resistance to its policy demands, soaring fiscal costs, and
    accumulating evidence of IMF policy failure.[13]*

The general public has not seen such "internal criticism" of
the IMF. If an outsider were to make the very same criticism, he
would be ostracized for being part of the radical fringe.

---

13   Felix, IMF Bailouts and Global Financial Flows, Vol. 3, No. 3, April 1998

So, conditionalities are instruments of forcing open markets in third-world countries, and of collecting defaulted debts owed by public and private organizations. The accumulating result of conditionalities is increasing resistance to such demands, bordering on hatred in many countries. The countries who can least afford it are saddled with soaring costs, additional debt and reduced national sovereignty.

Perhaps the most authoritative report on this topic was produced in 2002 by Axel Dreher of the Hamburg Institute of International Economics entitled *The Development and Implementation of IMF and World Bank Conditionality.*

Dreher notes that there was no consideration of conditionalities at the founding of the IMF, but rather they were gradually added in increasing numbers as the years passed and mostly by U.S. banking interests.[14] Conditionalities are arbitrary, unregulated, and imposed in varying degrees on different countries according to the whims of the negotiators. The recipient countries have little, if any, bargaining power.

This writer has observed several times that 1973, with the creation of the Trilateral Commission, was a pivotal year in the stampede to globalization. It is no surprise then that conditionalities became a standard business practice in 1974 with the introduction of the Extended Fund Facility (EFF).[15] EFF created lines of credit, or "credit tranches", that could be drawn on as needed by a troubled country, thus creating additional moral hazards as well.

Dreher also points out the tight coordination with the World Bank:

> *The reforms under IMF programs have mainly been designed by World Bank economists. Fund conditionality often was supportive of measures contained in Bank supported public enterprise reform operations. The selection of public enterprises to be reformed as well as the modalities and time table was developed by the Bank as well.[16]*

---

14   Dreher, The Development and Implementation of IMF and World Bank Conditionality, Hamburg Institute of International Economics 14,
15   Ibid. p. 9.
16   ibid, p. 17

So, we see that the IMF does not act alone in the application of conditionalities and in some cases, it is pointedly driven by the World Bank.

Dreher's meticulous research uncovered another interesting statistic: The most frequent condition included is bank privatization -- included in 35 percent of the programs analyzed![17] International bankers have always had disdain for banking operations run by governments instead of by private or corporate ownership. Thus, they have used the IMF and World Bank to force privatization of what remains in government hands in the third-world.

If all of this was not disturbing enough, Dreher informs us that there are direct connections between conditionalities imposed and various private banks who work in concert with the IMF and World Bank:

> *Since private creditors were willing to lend further only if IMF programs were in effect, the Fund's leverage was enhanced... since for crisis resolution sometimes more money is needed than can be provided by the IFIs, IMF and World Bank depend on these private creditors who should therefore be able to press for conditions which lie in their interest.[18]*

With the IMF, World Bank and other international banks forcing governments to run their countries in ways not of their choosing, and with the United States viewed as the primary driver of these organizations, it is no wonder that the third-world musters such intense hatred for the U.S. and for the self-interested globalization it exports wherever possible. The globalization process is most often anti-democratic and completely ineffective at accomplishing it's lofty stated goal of poverty reduction.

It should be plainly evident by now that the "can opener" for globalization to take place is the power of money. Borrowed money enslaves the borrower, and puts him at the mercy of the lender. When President Bill Clinton finally acknowledged the error of his ways during his affair with Monica Lewinski, he stated that it was for the absolutely worst of reasons: "Because I could." Why do these global financial organizations take such advantage of those

---

17   ibid. p. 18
18   ibid, p. 18

whom they systematically put in jeopardy? Because they can!

IMF Bailout of Asia

The Asian currency crisis came to a head in 1998, and the IMF was on the spot for a massive bailout. Vocal critics of the IMF at that time included George P. Schultz (member of the Trilateral Commission), William E. Simon (Secretary of the Treasury under Nixon and Ford) and Walter B. Wriston (former chairman of Citigroup/Citibank and member of the Council on Foreign Relations). They jointly wrote *Abolish the IMF?* for the Hoover Institution, where Shultz is also a distinguished fellow. The article states:

> *The $118 billion Asian bailout, which may rise to as much as $160 billion, is by far the largest ever undertaken by the IMF. A distant second was the 1995 Mexican bailout, which involved some $30 billion in loans, mostly from the IMF and the U.S. Treasury. The IMF's defenders often tout the Mexican bailout as a success because the Mexican government repaid the loans on schedule. But the Mexican people suffered a massive decline in their standard of living as a result of that crisis. As is typical when the IMF intervenes, the governments and the lenders were rescued but not the people.*[19]

Their scathing attack continues throughout the article, and concludes with

> *The IMF is ineffective, unnecessary, and obsolete. We do not need another IMF, as Mr. (George) Soros recommends. Once the Asian crisis is over, we should abolish the one we have.*[20]

It's interesting that these core members of the global elite are throwing stones at their own institution. What is outrageous is that they are completely side-stepping their own personal culpability for having used it to drive globalization with all of its ill side-effects. The fact that they succinctly describe the damage done by the IMF clearly dispenses their typical claim of "ignorance." Are they setting the stage to disband the IMF in favor of another, more powerful monetary authority? Time will tell.

19   Shultz, et. al, Who Needs the IMF?, Hoover Institution Public Policy Inquiry on the IMF
20   ibid.

Argentina: A Case Study of Privatization

In 2001, the IMF handed a bailout package to Argentina, valued at $8 billion. The major beneficiaries were the European megabanks, which held about 75 percent of the country's foreign debt. The money river flowed like this: IMF gives $8 billion (about $1.6 billion of which was tax money collected from hard working Americans) to Argentina; Argentina buys U.S. Treasury bills (U.S. gets the dollars back after being "monetized"); Argentina delivers Treasury Bills to creditor banks who graciously agree to retire their worthless Argentinian bonds.

Less than a decade earlier, the IMF and the World Bank backed Argentina in the largest water privatization project in the world. In 1993, Aquas Argentinas was formed between Argentina's water authority and a consortium that included the Suez group from France (largest private water company in the world) and Aquas de Barcelona of Spain. The new company covered a region populated by over 10 million inhabitants.

Now, after 10 years of higher water rates, decreased quality of water and sewage treatment, and neglected infrastructure improvements, the consortium is breaking its 30-year contract and pulling out. Bitterness between Aqua and government officials runs deep because of broken promises and political backlash.

The aftermath of Aqua Argentina is recorded in the November 21, 2005 online edition of the Guardian:

> More than 1 million residents in the rural Argentinian province of Santa Fe are facing an anxious wait to discover if their taps will still flow or their toilets flush over the next few weeks.

> Since 1995, the province has had its water supply and sewage services provided by a consortium led by the French multinational Suez; now the giant utility wants out, and plans to leave within the month.

> The decision, which follows the high-profile collapse of other water privatisation schemes in countries including Tanzania, Puerto Rico, the Philippines and Bolivia, has again raised questions about the viability of privatising utilities in the developing world.

Suez is also preparing an early departure from its formerly lucrative concession in the Argentine capital, Buenos Aires. The deal, struck in 1993, marked the largest water privatisation project in the world.

In both cases, the French utility is terminating its 30-year contract a third of the way through. Suez cannot get the concessions to turn a profit - at least not under the terms of its current agreements.

The French utility giant snapped up both service agreements in the mid-1990s when Argentina was undergoing a massive reform of its public sector, largely at the behest of the World Bank and other lending agencies.[21]

Aqua Argentina milked the market as long as it could, and then simply bailed out. And, why not? The profit dried up and it's not their country!

Global statistics show that some 460 million people around the world must rely on private water corporations like Aqua Argentina, compared to only 51 million in 1990. The IMF (and World Bank) levered the extra 400 million people into privatized contracts with water mega-companies from Europe and the U.S. Now that the cream has been skimmed off the top of the milk, these same companies are excusing themselves from the party -- leaving a shambles, angry customers and incapable governments still saddled with the billions of dollars of debt incurred (at their insistence) to start privatization in the first place.

[Note: In February 2003, CBC News in Canada produced an in depth report *Water for Profit: how multinationals are taking control of a public resource that included features and segments that were delivered across five days of broadcasting.*][22]

Conclusion

This report does not pretend to be an exhaustive analysis of the IMF. There are many facets, examples and case studies that could be explored. In fact, many critical analysis books have been written about the IMF. The object of this report was to show gen-

---

21   The trickle-away effect, The Guardian, November 21, 2005
22   CBC News, Water for Profit: how multinationals are taking control of a public resource

erally how the IMF fits into globalization as a critical member in the triad of global monetary powers: The IMF, the BIS and the World Bank.

Despite even establishment calls for the dissolution of the IMF, it continues to operate unhindered and with virtually no accountability. This is reminiscent of the BIS continuing to operate even after its dissolution was officially mandated after WWII.

For the purpose of this chapter, it is sufficient to conclude that...

- of the two founders of the IMF, one was an outright traitor to the U.S. and the other was a British citizen totally dedicated to globalism
- the IMF, in coordination with the BIS, tightly controls currencies and foreign exchange rates in the global economy
- the IMF is a channel for taxpayer money to be used to bail out private banks who made questionable loans to countries already saddled with too much debt
- the IMF uses conditionalities as a lever to force privatization of key and basic industries, such as banking, water, sewer and utilities
- conditionalities are often structured with help from the private banks who loan alongside of the IMF
- the policies of privatization accomplish just the opposite of what was promised
- the global elite are neither ignorant nor repentant of the distress the IMF has caused so many nations in the third-world
- when the public heat gets too hot, the global elite simply join the critics (thereby shunning all blame) while quietly creating new initiatives that allow them to get on with business -- that is, their business!

CHAPTER 2

THE WORLD BANK

Created at Bretton Woods in 1944, the World Bank has been dominated by international bankers, members of the Council on Foreign Relations and later by the Trilateral Commission. Corruption and self-interest run amok as public funds are converted into private hands by the billions.

According to The World Bank, it is,

> *a vital source of financial and technical assistance to developing countries around the world. We are not a bank in the common sense. We are made up of two unique development institutions owned by 184 member countries—the International Bank for Reconstruction and Development (IBRD) and the International Development Association (IDA). Each institution plays a different but supportive role in our mission of global poverty reduction and the improvement of living standards. The IBRD focuses on middle income and creditworthy poor countries, while IDA focuses on the poorest countries in the world. Together we provide low-interest loans, interest-free credit and grants to developing countries for education, health, infrastructure, communications and many other purposes.[23]*

High-minded words like "our mission of global poverty reduction and the improvement of living standards" would lead the reader to believe that the World Bank is some benevolent and global welfare organization. Why is it then, that The World Bank joins the International Monetary Fund and the World Trade Organization as organizations that people around the world just love to hate?

In reality, the World Bank carries its weight, along with the International Monetary Fund and the Bank for International Settlements, to forcibly integrate minor countries of the world into its own brand of capitalistic democracy.

World Bank Beginnings

A sibling of the IMF, the World Bank was born out of the U.N. Monetary and Financial Conference at Bretton Woods, New Hampshire in July, 1944. The original name given to the World Bank was the International Bank for Reconstruction and Development (IBRD) and reflects its original mission: to rebuild Europe after the devastation of World War II. The name "World Bank" was not actually adopted until 1975.

Both the IBRD and the IMF were created as independent specialized agencies of the United Nations, of which they remain to this day.

The word "Development" in the IBRD name was rather insignificant at the time because most of the southern hemisphere was still under colonial rule, with each colonial master responsible for the business activities in their respective countries.

Note: It is argued by some that there was an original desire by banking elites to put an end to colonialism by restructuring investment and trade patterns in colonized countries. This paper will not deal with this issue, but it should be noted that this has been exactly what has happened, in many cases being aided by the operations of the World Bank and the IMF.

As a "reconstruction" bank, however, the World Bank was impotent. It ultimately loaned only $497(US) million for reconstruction projects. The Marshall Plan, by contrast, became the true engine of the reconstruction of Europe by loaning over $41(US) billion by 1953.

The primary architects of the World Bank were Harry Dexter White and John Maynard Keynes, both of whom are summarized Global Banking: The International Monetary Fund (see article for complete details) as follows:

"Such is the moral fiber and intellectual credentials of the creators of the IMF [and the World Bank]: One was an English

ideologue economist with a markedly global bent, and the other a corrupt and high-ranking U.S. government official who was a top Soviet spy."[24]

Structure of the World Bank

Today, the World Bank consists of two primary units: The already-mentioned IBRD and the International Development Association (IDA), which was created in 1960.

The IBRD lends only to governments who are credit-worthy; in other words, there is an expectation that they will repay their loans. The IDA, by contrast, only lends to governments who are not credit-worthy and are usually the poorest nations. Together, they create a "one-two" punch in global lending to any government that they are able to talk into borrowing. The U.S. currently contributes about $1 billion per year of taxpayer funds to the IDA.

Three other affiliates combine with the World Bank, to be collectively called the World Bank Group:

- The International Finance Corporation (IFC) - Founded in 1956, lends directly to the private sector in developing counties.

- The Multilateral Investment Guarantee Agency (MIGA) -Founded in 1988, provides guarantees to investors in developing countries against losses caused by noncommercial risks.

- The International Center for Settlement of Investment Disputes (ICSID) - Founded in 1966, provides international facilities for conciliation and arbitration of investment disputes.

Headquarters for the World Bank is Washington, DC. It employs approximately 7,000 in the Washington complex, and another 3,000 in 109 offices scattered throughout member countries.

IBRD funds its lending operations by selling AAA-rated bonds and other debt instruments to other banks, pension funds, insurance companies and corporations around the world. By contrast, the IDA is funded by (taxpayer) contributions from mem-

---

24   The August Review, Global Banking: The International Monetary Fund.

ber countries. Annual levels of lending is roughly equal between IBRD and IDA. While the IFC generates its own capital in open markets, MIGA and ICSID receive the majority of their funding from the World Bank, much of which is taxpayer funded.

Ownership of the World Bank consists of voting shares held by member countries, according to size and contributions. Currently, the U.S. is the largest shareholder with 16.4 percent of total votes. The next largest voting blocks are Japan (7.9 percent) and Germany (4.5 percent). Because major decisions require an 85 percent super-majority vote, the U.S. can effectively veto any change (100% -16.4% = 83.6%).

American Hegemony

It should be noted that the United Nations is headquartered in the United States, on land originally donated to it by David Rockefeller. The Bretton Woods Conference was held in New Hampshire. Every president of the World Bank has hailed from the United States. It is no wonder that the rest of the world views the World Bank as an American operation.

There has been an unwritten but traditional rule that the World Bank president will always be an American, while the president of the IMF is European. (A recent exception to this is the current IMF president, who is a Canadian.)

It is instructive to review the past presidents of the World Bank, because it demonstrates which elite cabal is really in control of World Bank operations. In turn, this will point strongly to the real beneficiaries of the World Bank hegemony. The complete biographies and accomplishments of these men far exceed the available space in this report, so only a few highlights are noted.

1. Eugene Meyer. June to December, 1946. Chairman, Board of Governors of the Federal Reserve from 1930-1933; owner of the Washington Post; Member, Council on Foreign Relations; agent of Lazard Freres, Brown Brothers, Harriman; appointed head of the War Finance Corporation during WWI by Woodrow Wilson.

2. John J. McCloy. March 1947 to April 1949. Member and chair of the Council on Foreign Relations; Chairman, Ford Foundation; Chairman, Chase Manhattan Bank; lawyer whose firm was council to Chase Manhattan Bank.

3. Eugene Black. July 1949 to December 1962. Chairman, Board of Directors for the Federal Reserve System (1933-34); senior vice president of Chase Manhattan Bank; Member, Council on Foreign Relations; member of Bilderbergers; created the International Finance Corporation and the International Development Association at the World Bank.

4. George Woods. January 1963 to March 1968. Vice president of Harris, Forbes & Co.; vice president of Chase Bank; vice president of and board member of First Boston Corp. (one of the largest U.S. investment banking firms).

5. Robert Strange McNamara. April 1968 to June 1981. President and director of Ford Motor Company; Secretary of Defense in the Kennedy and Johnson administrations; member of Trilateral Commission, Council on Foreign Relations and Bilderbergers; honorary council trustee of Aspen Institute. Personally negotiated China's entrance into the World Bank.

6. A.W. Clausen. July 1981 to June 1986. President, CEO and chairman of Bank of America; member, Trilateral Commission; member, Bretton-Woods Committee.

7. Barber B. Conable. July 1986 to August 1991. Member of U.S. House of Representatives from 1965 to 1985; member Trilateral Commission and Council on Foreign Relations; senior fellow, American Enterprise Institute; board member, New York Stock Exchange; member, Commission on Global Governance.

8. Lewis T. Preston. September 1991 to May 1995. President, CEO and chairman of J.P. Morgan & Co., and chairman of the executive committee; vice president of Morgan Guaranty Trust Co.; member and treasurer of Council on Foreign Relations; director of General Electric.

9. James D. Wolfensohn. June 1995 to 2005 Executive partner and head of the investment banking department, Salomon Brothers (New York); executive deputy chairman and managing director, Schroders Ltd. (London); director, Rockefeller Foundation; board member, Rockefeller University; honorary trustee, Brookings Institution; Director, Population Council (founded by John D. Rockefeller); member, Council on Foreign

Relations.

10. Paul Wolfowitz. 2005 - present. Deputy Secretary of Defense (2001-2005); member, Trilateral Commission; member, Council on Foreign Relations; member, Bilderbergers; director of the neocon flagship, Project for the New American Century (PNAC); member of the elite "Vulcans" group that advised George W. Bush on foreign policy during the 2000 presidential elections (other neocon members included Condoleezza Rice, Colin Powell and Richard Perle); member of and frequent speaker at Social Democrats USA (successor to the Socialist Party of America).

An important pattern emerges here. These men frame a 50-year time period stretching from 1946 to 2006. The early players have long since passed away. There was no social connection between the early and latter presidents. Yet, seven out of ten are members of the Council on Foreign Relations; four are members of the Trilateral Commission, seven have major global bank affiliations (Chase Manhattan, J.P. Morgan, Bank of America, First Boston, Brown Brothers, Harriman, Salomon Brothers, Federal Reserve), and four men were directly connected to Rockefeller interests.

A detailed analysis is not required to see the pattern emerge: Global bankers (the same old crowd) and their related global proxies, have completely dominated the World Bank for its entire history. Collectively and individually, they have always operated purposefully and consistently for their own self-interested, financial gain. Why would anyone expect even one of them to act out of character (e.g., be concerned for world poverty) while directing the helm of the World Bank?

Purposes of convenience

Whatever the true purposes of the World Bank and IMF might have been, the publicly displayed purposes have changed when it was convenient and necessary.

In 1944, reconstruction of war torn countries after WW II was the important issue.

When the Bank demonstrated its impotence by loaning only a pittance of less than $500 million, it changed its pubic image by positioning itself as a check and balance to the expansion of communism. Without the World Bank to engage all of the lesser countries of the world who were susceptible to communist influence, communism might spread and ultimately threaten to end the cold war with an ugly nuclear Holocaust.

Public and legislative sentiment ultimately fizzled and the Bank was again under heavy criticism when Robert Strange McNamara was appointed president.

Poverty Reduction: Trojan Horse

As noted above, McNamara was president of the World Bank from 1968 through 1981. He was also among the original membership of the Trilateral Commission, founded in 1973 by Rockefeller and Brzezinski, and was widely considered to be a central figure in the global elite of his day.

It was McNamara who caused the focus of the World Bank to fall on poverty and poverty reduction. This has essentially remained the siren call right into the present. This was a brilliant maneuver because who would ever say they are anti-poor or pro-poverty? Any attack on the Bank would thus be viewed as an attack on poverty relief itself. From 1968 onward, the battle cry of the Bank has been "eliminate poverty."

This is clearly seen on the About Us page of the World Bank web site, where these words are prominently displayed:

"Each institution (IBRD and IDA) plays a different but supportive role in our mission of global poverty reduction and the improvement of living standards." [emphasis added]

However, Article I of The Articles of Agreement of the IBRD, as amended on February 16, 1989, state its official Purposes as follows:

(i) To assist in the reconstruction and development of territories of members by facilitating the investment of capital for productive purposes, including the restoration of economies destroyed or disrupted by war, the reconversion of productive facilities to peacetime needs and the encouragement of the development of productive facilities and resources in less developed countries.

(ii) To promote private foreign investment by means of guarantees or participations in loans and other investments made by private investors; and when private capital is not available on reasonable terms, to supplement private investment by providing, on suitable conditions, finance for productive purposes out of its own capital, funds raised by it and its other resources.

(iii) To promote the long-range balanced growth of international trade and the maintenance of equilibrium in balances of payments by encouraging international investment for the development of the productive resources of members, thereby assisting in raising productivity, the standard of living and conditions of labor in their territories.

(iv) To arrange the loans made or guaranteed by it in relation to international loans through other channels so that the more useful and urgent projects, large and small alike, will be dealt with first.

(v) To conduct its operations with due regard to the effect of international investment on business conditions in the territories of members and, in the immediate postwar years, to assist in bringing about a smooth transition from a wartime to a peacetime economy.

The Bank shall be guided in all its decisions by the purposes set forth above.[25]

Note that the word "poverty" does not appear even once. The reason is clear: Whatever "business as usual" might be with the Bank, it has nothing to do with poverty or poverty reduction. Rather, the Bank is in business to loan money by stimulating borrowing demand in developing countries, with a view to increasing international trade. The primary beneficiaries of international trade are the global corporations, and the poor are actually poorer as a result.

This hypocrisy was noted even by Nobel laureate and former World Bank chief economist, Joseph Stiglitz, as late as 2002:

As far as these 'client countries' were concerned, it was a charade in which the politicians pretended to do something to redress the problems [of poverty] while financial interests

---

worked to preserve as much of the status quo as they could.[26]

Liberalization and Structural Adjustments

When Alden Clausen (also an original member of the Trilateral Commission) took over the reins from Robert McNamara in 1981, a massive shakeup in the bank occurred. As Stiglitz noted,

"In the early 1980's a purge occurred inside the World Bank, in its research department, which guided the Bank's thinking and direction."[27]

Clausen, a true core member of the global elite, brought in a new chief economist with radical new ideas:

"...Ann Krueger, an international trade specialist, best known for her work on 'rent seeking' -- how special interests use tariffs and other protectionist measures to increase their incomes at the expense of others... **Krueger saw government as the problem. Free markets were the solution to the problems of developing countries.***"*[28] *[emphasis added]*

This was precisely the time when so-called liberalization policies and Structural Adjustments were forcefully implemented as a means of forcing countries to privatize industries. If governments were the problem, then they should turn over areas of critical infrastructure to private multinational corporations which, according to Krueger, could perform better and more efficiently than bureaucratic government bodies.

Not surprisingly, most of the career staff economists left the Bank in the early 1980's in protest over Clausen and Krueger's policies.

How the Money Laundry Works

The mechanism and operation of Structural Adjustments, along with the tight cooperation between the IMF and the World Bank, was adequately covered in The August Review's Global Banking: The International Monetary Fund. The following well-documented example will be the "picture worth a thousand words" in the Review's effort to profile self-serving Bank and

---

26   Stiglitz, Globalization and its Discontents (Norton, 2002), p. 234
27   ibid, p. 13.
28   ibid.

global corporate policies. It also demonstrates the "tag-team" approach used by the Bank and IMF in the prying open of closed markets in uncooperative countries. It's a rather tangled story, but careful reading will produce understanding of how the "system" works.

Water Wars

In 1998, the IMF approved a loan of $138 million for Bolivia it described as designed to help the country control inflation and stabilize its domestic economy. The loan was contingent upon Bolivia's adoption of a series of "structural reforms," including Privatization of "all remaining public enterprises," including water services. Once these loans were approved, Bolivia was under intense pressure from the World Bank to ensure that no public subsidies for water existed and that all water projects would be run on a "cost recovery" basis, meaning that citizens must pay the full construction, financing, operation and maintenance costs of a water project. Because water is an essential human need and is crucial for agriculture, cost recovery pricing is unusual, even in the developed world.

In this context, Cochabamba, the third largest city in Bolivia, put its water works up for sale in late 1999.

Only one entity, a consortium led by Bechtel subsidiary Aguas del Tunari, offered a bid, and it was awarded a 40-year concession to provide water. The exact details of the negotiation were kept secret, and Bechtel claimed that the numbers within the contract are "intellectual property." But, it later came to light that the price included the financing by Cochabamba's citizens of a part of a huge dam construction project being undertaken by Bechtel, even though water from the Misicuni Dam Project would be 600% more expensive than alternative water sources. Cochabambans were also required to pay Bechtel a contractually guaranteed 15% profit, meaning that the people of Cochabamba were asked to pay for investments while the private sector got the profits.

Immediately upon receiving the concession, the company

raised water rates by as much as 400% in some instances. These increases came in an area where the minimum wage is less than $100 a month. After the price hike, self-employed men and women were estimated to pay one quarter of their monthly earnings for water.

The city's residents were outraged. In January of 2000, a broad coalition called the Coordination for the Defense of Water and Life, or simply La Coordinadora, led by a local worker, Oscar Olivera, called for peaceful demonstrations. Cochabamba was shut down for four days by a general strike and transportation stoppage, but the demonstrations stopped once the government promised to intervene to lower water rates. However, when there were no results in February, the demonstrations started again. This time, however, demonstrators were met with tear gas and police opposition, leaving 175 injured and two youths blinded.

The threat that privatization of public services under GATS (General Agreement on Trade in Services) poses to democracy were demonstrated in March 2000. La Coordinadora held an unofficial referendum, counted nearly 50,000 votes, and announced that 96% of the respondents favored the cancellation of the contract with Aguas del Tunari. They were told by the water company that there was nothing to negotiate.

On April 4, the residents of the city returned to the streets, shutting down the city. Again, they were met with police resistance, and on April 8, the government declared martial law. The Bolivian military shot a 17-year-old protester in the face, killing him. However, the protests continued, and, on April 10, the government relented, signing an accord that agreed to the demand of the protesters to reverse the water concession. The people of Cochabamba took back their water.

Unfortunately, this inspiring story didn't simply end with the victory for the people of Cochabamba. On February 25, 2002, Bechtel filed a grievance using investor protections granted in a Bolivia-Netherlands Bilateral Investment Agreement at the World Bank, demanding a $25 million dollar payment as *compensation for lost profits.*[29]

Note: Bechtel Engineering is the largest civil engineering company in the world. It is privately owned by the Bechtel family. For many years, general counsel (and vice-president) for Bechtel was none other than original Trilateral Commission member Caspar Weinberger.

Since then, the World Bank has granted additional "poverty reduction" loans to Bolivia. Carefully read the Bank's current (2006) assessment on Bolivia found on its web site:

"Bolivia is experiencing a time of difficulty and uncertainty. In recent months, various political and social disturbances have escalated with serious consequences, culminating in the resignation of President Gonzalo Sánchez de Lozada in October 2003, and the appointment of Vice-President Carlos Mesa as President. The current administration inherits a difficult economic, political and social climate, which is compounded by long-term issues, such as profound inequality, an economy that has been adversely affected by the region's recent economic slump, and widespread public disenchantment with corruption."[30]

Political and social disturbances? Difficult economic, political and social climate? Profound inequality? Widespread disenchantment with corruption? It leaves one speechless.

So, in the case of Bolivia, we see the following in operation:

- An IMF loan is made to Bolivia, with conditionalities
- The World Bank steps in to enforce the conditionalities and impose structural adjustments
- The World Bank loans "development" funds to Bolivia, and simultaneously brings in private bank consortiums to fund the various projects that Bechtel had in mind.
- Bechtel makes a sole-source bid, and it is accepted.
- The water project ends in total failure and Bechtel gets kicked out after extreme political pressure from consumers.
- Bechtel files a "lost profit" claim according to a pre-

29   Wallach, Whose Trade Organization? (The New Press, 2004), p.125.
30   World Bank web site, Bolivia Country Brief

negotiated "insurance guarantee" with the World Bank Group (MIGA, see above.)

- If Bechtel wins its claim, it will be paid off with taxpayer money contributed by member countries.
- Undoubtedly, any loans from private-sector banks that later turn sour, will be bailed-out with taxpayer funds as well.

This kind of operation is brazen stealing (albeit perhaps legally) of funds from everyone in sight: Bolivia, the city of Cochabamba, the people of Cochabamba, U.S. taxpayers. The only beneficiaries are Bechtel, the commercial banks and a few corrupt politicians who got their customary bribes and kickbacks.

A penetrating question remains to be answered: When did Bechtel first set their sights on the Bolivia deal? Did Bechtel have a role in suggesting or creating the conditionalities and Structural Adjustments specified by the World Bank in the first place? If so, there would be grounds for criminal investigation.

It is not likely that the World Bank will tell us, because of its very secretive inner workings. Even Stiglitz has noted,

"The IMF and World Bank still have disclosure standards far weaker than those of governments in democracies like the United States, or Sweden or Canada. They attempt to hide critical reports; it is only their inability to prevent leaks that often forces the eventual disclosure."[31]

Corruption

The World Bank has received accusations of corruption for many years. Since the Bank is an independent specialized agency of the United Nations and considering the old adage, "The fruit doesn't fall far from the tree", this might not come as a surprise to most. The United Nations has a major and documented track record on corruption of every conceivable sort. It would be too simplistic to just leave it at that.

In May, 2004, Sen. Richard Lugar (R-Indiana), as Chairman of the Foreign Relations Committee, kicked off the most recent inquiry into corruption related to the activities of the multilateral

---

31   Stiglitz, op. cit., p. 234.

development banks, of which the World Bank is foremost.

The heads of the various development banks were invited to testify (voluntarily) before the Committee. According to Sen. Lugar, James Wolfensohn "declined the invitation, citing the established practice of Bank officials not to testify before the legislatures of their numerous member countries."

Witnesses before the Committee testified that as much as $100 billion may have been lost to corruption in World Bank lending projects.

In Sen. Lugar's opening remarks, he points out that the entire history of the World Bank is suspect, with between 5 percent and 25 percent of all lending being lost to corruption.

> *"But corruption remains a serious problem. Dr. Jeffrey Winters of Northwestern University, who will testify before us today, estimates that the World Bank 'has participated mostly passively in the corruption of roughly $100 billion of its loan funds intended for development.' Other experts estimate that between 5 percent and 25 percent of the $525 billion that the World Bank has lent since 1946 has been misused. This is equivalent to between $26 billion and $130 billion. Even if corruption is at the low end of estimates, millions of people living in poverty may have lost opportunities to improve their health, education, and economic condition."[32]*

One must wonder why World Bank officials have been so sloppy and careless with taxpayer dollars. Even further, one must wonder if the corruption was a necessity to achieve the underlying purposes of the Bank, that is, to create bogus and unwanted projects in order to "stimulate" trade.

Sen. Lugar continued his opening remarks,

> *"Corruption thwarts development efforts in many ways. Bribes can influence important bank decisions on projects and on contractors. Misuse of funds can inflate project costs, deny needed assistance to the poor, and cause projects to fail. Stolen money may prop up dictatorships and finance human rights abuses. Moreover, when developing countries lose de-*

---

32   Lugar, U.S. Senate Website, $100 billion may have been lost to World Bank Corruption, May 13, 2004.

velopment bank funds through corruption, the taxpayers in those poor countries are still obligated to repay the development banks. So, not only are the impoverished cheated out of development benefits, they are left to repay the resulting debts to the banks."[33]

It has not been determined which Bank employees might have taken bribes in exchange for influence, but one can be sure that any deal starting with corruption only has one direction to go -- down. In the end, it is helpless individuals who are left holding the bag. The incurred debts and failed projects just add to the impoverishment of already poor people.

This is not to say that charges of corruption at the World Bank are modern revelations only. In 1994, marking the 50th anniversary of its creation at Bretton Woods, South End Press released "50 Years is Enough: The Case Against the World Bank and the International Monetary Fund,." edited by Kevin Danaher. The book details official Bank and IMF reports that reveal the same kind of corruption back then. In addition, it revealed different types of corruption, for instance,

"Beyond the wasted money and the environmental devastation, there was an even more sinister side to the Bank during the McNamara years: the World Bank's predilection for increasing support to military regimes that tortured and murdered their subjects, sometimes immediately after the violent overthrow of more democratic governments. In 1979, Senator James Abourezk (D-South Dakota) denounced the bank on the Senate floor, noting that the Bank was increasing 'loans to four newly repressive governments [Chile, Uruguay, Argentina and the Philippines] twice as fast as all others.' He noted that 15 of the world's most repressive governments would receive a third of all World Bank loan commitments in 1979, and that Congress and the Carter administration had cut off bilateral aid to four of the 15 -- Argentina, Chile, Uruguay and Ethiopia -- for flagrant human rights violations. He blasted the Bank's 'excessive secretiveness' and reminded his colleagues that 'we vote the money, yet we do not know

---

33   ibid.

where it goes.'" [34]

The text speaks for itself and needs no comment. Readers of this chapter will likely have a better understanding of where the money went!

Conclusions

This report does not pretend to be an exhaustive analysis of the World Bank. There are many facets, examples and case studies that could be explored. In fact, many critical and analytical books have been written about the World Bank. The object of this report was to show how the World Bank fits into globalization as a central member in the triad of global monetary powers: The IMF, the BIS and the World Bank.

The World Bank is likely to continue to operate despite any amount of political flack or public protest. Such is the pattern of elitist-dominated institutions. Such is the history of the International Monetary Fund and the Bank for International Settlements.

It is sufficient to conclude that...

- of the two architects of the World Bank, one was a top Soviet communist agent (Harry Dexter White) and the other was a British ideologue (John Maynard Keynes) totally dedicated to globalism (See Global Banking: The International Monetary Fundfor more details on White and Keynes)
- From the beginning, the Bank has been dominated by international banking interests and members of the Council on Foreign Relations and later by the Trilateral Commission
- the cry of "poverty reduction" is a sham to conceal the recycling of billions of taxpayer dollars, if not trillions, into private hands
- the cry of "poverty reduction" defuses critics of the Bank as being anti-poor and pro-poverty
- corruption at the World Bank goes back decades, if not

---

34   Danaher, 50 Years is Enough: The Case Against the World Bank and the International Monetary Fund, (South End Press, 1994), p. 10

all the way to the very beginning.

CHAPTER 3

THE BANK FOR INTERNATIONAL SETTLEMENTS

When David Rockefeller and Zbigniew Brzezinski founded the Trilateral Commission in 1973, the intent was to create a "New International Economic Order" (NIEO). To this end, they brought together 300 elite corporate, political and academic leaders from North America, Japan and Europe.

Few people believed us when we wrote about their nefarious plans back then. Now, we look back and clearly see that they did what they said they were going to do... globalism is upon us like an 8.6 magnitude earthquake.

The question is, "How did they do it?" Keep in mind, they had no public mandate from any country in the world. They didn't have the raw political muscle, especially in democratic countries where voting is allowed. They didn't have global dictatorial powers.

Indeed, how did they do it?

The answer is the Bank for International Settlements (BIS), self-described as the "central bank for central bankers", that controls the vast global banking system with the precision of a Swiss watch.

This report offers a concise summation of BIS history, structure and current activities.

The famous currency expert Dr. Franz Pick once stated, "The destiny of the currency is, and always will be, the destiny of a nation."

With the advent of rampant globalization, this concept can certainly be given a global context as well: "The destiny of currencies are, and always will be, the destiny of the world."

Even though the BIS is the oldest international banking operation in the world, it is a low profile organization, shunning all publicity and notoriety. As a result, there is very little critical analysis written about this important financial organization. Further, much of what has been written about it is tainted by its own self-effacing literature.

The BIS can be compared to a stealth bomber. It flies high and fast, is undetected, has a small crew and carries a huge payload. By contrast, however, the bomber answers to a chain of command and must be refueled by outside sources. The BIS, as we shall see, is not accountable to any public authority and operates with complete autonomy and self-sufficiency.

Leading up to Founding

As we will see, the BIS was founded in 1930 during a very troubled time in history. Some knowledge of that history is critical to understanding why the BIS was created, and for whose benefit.

There are three figures that play prominently in the founding of the BIS: Charles G. Dawes, Owen D. Young and Hjalmar Schacht of Germany.

Charles G. Dawes was director of the U.S. Bureau of the Budget in 1921, and served on the Allied Reparations Commission starting in 1923. His latter work on "stabilizing Germany's economy" earned him the Nobel Peace Prize in 1925. After being elected Vice President under President Calvin Coolidge from 1925-1929, and appointed Ambassador to England in 1931, he resumed his personal banking career in 1932 as chairman of the board of the City National Bank and Trust in Chicago, where he remained until his death in 1951.

Owen D Young was an American industrialist. He founded RCA (Radio Corporation of America) in 1919 and was its chairman until 1933. He also served as the chairman of General Electric from 1922 until 1939. In 1932, Young sought the democratic presidential nomination, but lost to Franklin Delano Roosevelt.

More on Hjalmar Schacht later.

In the aftermath of World War I and the impending collapse of the German economy and political structure, a plan was needed to rescue and restore Germany, which would also insulate other economies in Europe from being affected adversely.

The Versailles Treaty of 1919 (which officially ended WWI) had imposed a very heavy reparations burden on Germany, which required a repayment schedule of 132 billion gold marks per year. Most historians agree that the economic upheaval caused in Germany by the Versailles Treaty eventually led to Adolph Hitler's rise to power.

In 1924 the Allies appointed a committee of international bankers, led by Charles G. Dawes (and accompanied by J.P. Morgan agent, Owen Young), to develop a plan to get reparations payments back on track. Historian Carroll Quigley noted that the Dawes Plan was "largely a J.P. Morgan production"[35] The plan called for $800 million in foreign loans to be arranged for Germany in order to rebuild its economy.

In 1924, Dawes was chairman of the Allied Committee of Experts, hence, the "Dawes Plan." He was replaced as chairman by Owen Young in 1929, with direct support by J.P. Morgan. The "Young Plan" of 1928 put more teeth into the Dawes Plan, which many viewed as a strategy to subvert virtually all German assets to back a huge mortgage held by the United States bankers.

Neither Dawes nor Young represented anything more than banking interests. After all, WWI was fought by governments using borrowed money made possible by the international banking community. The banks had a vested interest in having those loans repaid!

In 1924, the president of Reichsbank (Germany's central bank at that time) was Hjalmar Schacht. He had already had a prominent role in creating the Dawes Plan, along with German industrialist Fritz Thyssen and other prominent German bankers and industrialists.

The Young Plan was so odious to the Germans that many credit it as a precondition to Hitler's rise to power. Fritz Thyssen, a leading Nazi Industrialist, stated

"I turned to the National socialist party only after I became

---

35   Quigley, Tragedy & Hope, (MacMillan, 1966), p.308

convinced that the fight against the Young Plan was unavoid-able if complete collapse of Germany was to be prevented." [36]

Some historians too quickly credit Owen Young as the idea-man for the Bank for International Settlements. It was actually Hjalmar Schacht who first proposed the idea[37], which was then carried forward by the same group of international bankers who brought us the Dawes and Young Plans.

It is not necessary to jump to conclusions as to the intent of these elite bankers, so we will instead defer to the insight of re-nowned Georgetown historian, Carroll Quigley:

> *"The Power of financial capitalism had another far reaching plan, nothing less than to create a world system of financial control in private hands able to dominate the political system of each country and the economy of the world as a whole. This system was to be controlled in a feudalistic fashion by the central banks of the world acting in concert, by secret agree-ments arrived at in frequent meetings and conferences. **The apex of the system was to be the Bank for International Settlements in Basle, Switzerland, a private bank owned and controlled by the world's central banks, which were themselves private corporations.**Each central bank, in the hands of men like Montagu Norman of the Bank of England, Benjamin Strong of the New York Federal Reserve Bank, Charles Rist of the Bank of France, and Hjalmar Schacht of the Reichsbank, sought to dominate its government by its ability to control treasury loans, to manipulate foreign exchanges, to influence the level of economic activity in the country, and to influence co-operative politicians by subsequent rewards in the business world."*[38] [Bold emphasis added]

So here we have a brief sketch of what led up to the founding of the BIS. Now we can examine the nuts and bolts of how the BIS was actually put together.

---

36   Edgar B Nixon, ec., Franklin D. Roosevelt and Foreign Affairs, Volume III (Cambridge: Balknap Press, 1969) p. 456

37   Sutton, Wall Street and the Rise of Hitler, (GSC & Associates, 2002) p. 26.

38   Quigley, op cit, p. 324

The Hague Agreement of 1930

The formation of the BIS was agreed upon by its constituent central banks in the so-called Hague Agreement on January 20, 1930, and was in operation shortly thereafter. According to the Agreement,

The duly authorised representatives of the governments of Germany, of Belgium, of France, of the United Kingdom of Great Britain and Northern Ireland, of Italy and of Japan of the one part; the duly authorised representatives of the government of the Swiss Confederation of the other part assembled at the Hague Conference in the month of January, 1930, have agreed on the following:

> *Article 1. Switzerland undertakes to grant to the Bank for International Settlements, without delay, the following Constituent Charter having force of law: not to abrogate this Charter, not to amend or add to it, and not to sanction amendments to the Statutes of the Bank referred to in Paragraph 4 of the Charter otherwise than in agreement with the other signatory Governments.*[39]

As we will see, German reparation payments (or lack thereof) had little to do with the founding of the BIS, although this is the weak explanation given since its founding. Of course, Germany would make a single payment to the BIS, which in turn would deposit the funds into the respective central bank accounts of the nations to whom payments were due. The net amount that Germany actually paid was very small.

The original founding documents of the BIS have little to say about Germany, however, and we can look directly to the BIS itself to see its original purpose:

> *The objects of the Bank are: to promote the co-operation of central banks and to provide additional facilities for international operations; and to act as trustees or agent in regard to international financial settlements entrusted to it under agreements with the parties concerned.*[40]

39　BIS web site, Extracts from the Hague Convention, www.bis.org/about/conv-ex.htm.
40　BIS, Statutes of the Bank for International Settlements Article 3 [as if January 1930, text as amended on March 10, 2003], Basic Texts (Basle, August 2003), p. 7-8.

Virtually every in-print reference to the BIS, including their own documents, consistently refer to it as "the central banker's central bank."

So, the BIS was established by an international charter and was headquartered in Basle, Switzerland.

BIS Ownership

According to James C. Baker, pro-BIS author of The Bank for International Settlements: Evolution and Evaluation, "The BIS was formed with funding by the central banks of six nations, Belgium, France, Germany, Italy, Japan, and the United Kingdom. In addition, three private international banks from the United States also assisted in financing the establishment of the BIS."[41]

Each nation's central bank subscribed to 16,000 shares. The U.S. central bank, the Federal Reserve, did not join the BIS, but the three U.S. banks that participated got 16,000 shares each. Thus, U.S. representation at the BIS was three times that of any other nation. Who were these private banks? Not surprisingly, they were J.P. Morgan & Company, First National Bank of New York and First National Bank of Chicago.

On January 8, 2001, an Extraordinary General Meeting of the BIS approved a proposal that restricted ownership of BIS shares to central banks. Some 13.7% of all shares were in private hands at that time, and the repurchase was accomplished with a cash outlay of $724,956,050. The price of $10,000 per share was over twice the book value of $4,850.

It is not certain what the repurchase accomplished. The BIS claimed that it was to correct a conflict of interest between private shareholders and BIS goals, but it offered no specifics. It was not a voting issue, however, because private owners were not allowed to vote their shares.[42]

Sovereignty and Secrecy

It is not surprising that the BIS, its offices, employees, directors and members share an incredible immunity from virtually

---

41   Baker, The Bank for International Settlements: Evolution and Evaluation, (Quorum, 2002), p. 20.
42   ibid.

all regulation, scrutiny and accountability.

In 1931, central bankers and their constituents were fed up with government meddling in world financial affairs. Politicians were viewed mostly with contempt, unless it was one of their own who was the politician. Thus, the BIS offered them a once-and-for-all opportunity to set up the "apex" the way they really wanted it -- private. They demanded these conditions and got what they demanded.

A quick summary of their immunity, explained further below, includes:

- diplomatic immunity for persons and what they carry with them (i.e., diplomatic pouches)
- no taxation on any transactions, including salaries paid to employees
- embassy-type immunity for all buildings and/or offices operated by the BIS
- no oversight or knowledge of operations by any government authority
- freedom from immigration restrictions
- freedom to encrypt any and all communications of any sort
- freedom from any legal jurisdiction.[43]

Further, members of the BIS board of directors (for instance, Alan Greenspan) are individually granted special benefits:

- immunity from arrest or imprisonment and immunity from seizure of their personal baggage, save in flagrant cases of criminal offense;
- inviolability of all papers and documents;
- immunity from jurisdiction, even after their mission has been accomplished, for acts carried out in the discharge of their duties, including words spoken and writings;
- exemption for themselves, their spouses and children from any immigration restrictions, from any formalities concerning the registration of aliens and from any obli-

---

43   BIS, Protocol Regarding the Immunities of the Bank for International Settlements, Basic Texts, (Basle, August 2003), p. 33.

gations relating to national service in Switzerland

- the right to use codes in official communications or to receive or send documents or correspondence by means of couriers or diplomatic bags.[44]

Lastly, all remaining officials and employees of the BIS have the following immunities:

- immunity from jurisdiction for acts accomplished in the discharge of their duties, including words spoken and writings, **even after such persons have ceased to be Officials of the Bank**; [bold emphasis added]
- exemption from all Federal, cantonal and communal taxes on salaries, fees and allowances paid to them by the Bank
- exempt from Swiss national obligations, freedom for spouses and family members from immigration restrictions, transfer assets and properties including internationally with the same degree of benefit as Officials of other international organizations.[45]

Of course, a corporate charter can say anything it wants to say and still be subject to outside authorities. Nevertheless, these were the immunities practiced and enjoyed from 1930 onward. On February 10, 1987, a more formal acknowledgement called the "Headquarters Agreement" was executed between the BIS and the Swiss Federal Council and basically clarified and reiterated what we already knew:

Article 2

Inviolability

- *The buildings or parts of buildings and surrounding land which, whoever may be the owner thereof, are used for the purposes of the Bank shall be inviolable. No agent of the Swiss public authorities may enter therein without the express consent of the Bank. Only the President, the General Manager of the Bank, or their duly authorised representative shall be competent to waive such inviolability.*

---

44   ibid, Article 12, p.43.
45   ibid, p. 44

- *The archives of the Bank and, in general, all documents and any data media belonging to the Bank or in its possession, shall be inviolable at all times and in all places.*

- *The Bank shall exercise supervision of and police power over its premises.*

Article 4
Immunity from jurisdiction and execution

- *The Bank shall enjoy immunity from criminal and administrative jurisdiction, save to the extent that such immunity is formally waived in individual cases by the President, the General Manager of the Bank, or their duly authorised representative.*

- *The assets of the Bank may be subject to measures of compulsory execution for enforcing monetary claims. On the other hand, **all deposits entrusted to the Bank, all claims against the Bank and the shares issued by the Bank shall, without the prior agreement of the Bank, be immune from seizure or other measures of compulsory execution and sequestration, particularly of attachment within the meaning of Swiss law.**[46]* [bold emphasis added]

Day-to-Day Operations

Acting as a central bank, the BIS has sweeping powers to do anything for its own account or for the account of its member central banks. It is like a two-way power-of-attorney: any party can act as agent for any other party.

Article 21 of the original BIS statutes define day-to-day operations:

1. buying and selling of gold coin or bullion for its own account or for the account of central banks;

2. holding gold for its own account under reserve in central banks;

---

46   BIS, Extracts from the Headquarters Agreement, www.bis.org/about/hq-ex.htm.

3. accepting the supervision of gold for the account of central banks;

4. making advances to or borrowing from central banks against gold, bills of exchange, and other short-term obligations of prime liquidity or other approved securities;

5. discounting, rediscounting, purchasing, or selling with or without its endorsement bills of exchange, checks, and other short-term obligations of prime liquidity;

6. buying and selling foreign exchange for its own account or for the account of central banks;

7. buying and selling negotiable securities other than shares for its own account or for the account of central banks;

8. discounting for central banks bills taken from their portfolio and rediscounting with central banks bills taken from its own portfolio;

9. opening and maintaining current or deposit accounts with central banks;

10. accepting deposits from central banks on current or deposit account;

11. accepting deposits in connection with trustee agreements that may be made between the BIS and governments in connection with international settlements.;

12. accepting such other deposits that, as in the opinion of the Board of the BIS, come within the scope of the BIS functions.[47]

The BIS also may:

1. act as agent or correspondent for any central bank

2. arrange with any central bank for the latter to act as its agent or correspondent;

3. enter into agreements to act as trustee or agent in connection with international settlements, provided that such agreements will not encroach on the obligations of the BIS toward any third parties.[48]

---

47   Baker, op cit, p. 26-27.
48   ibid. p. 27.

Why is "agency" an important issue? Because any member of the network can obscure transactions from onlookers. For instance, if Brown Brothers, Harriman wanted to transfer money to a company in Nazi Germany during WWII (which was not "politically correct" at that time), they would first transfer the funds to the BIS thus putting the transaction under the cloak of secrecy and immunity that is enjoyed by the BIS but not by Brown Brothers, Harriman. (Such laundering of Wall Street money was painstakingly noted in *Wall Street and the Rise of Hitler*, by Antony C. Sutton.)

There are a few things that the BIS cannot do. For instance, it does not accept deposits from, or provide financial services to, private individuals or corporate entities. It is also not permitted to make advances to governments or open current accounts in their name.[49] These restrictions are easily understood when one considers that each central bank has an exclusive franchise to loan money to their respective government. For instance, the U.S. Federal Reserve does not loan money to the government of Canada. In like manner, central banks do not loan money directly to the private or corporate clients of their member banks.

How Decisions are Made

The board of directors consist of the heads of certain member central banks. Currently, these are:

Nout H E M Wellink, Amsterdam (Chairman of the Board of Directors)

Hans Tietmeyer, Frankfurt am Main (Vice-Chairman)

Axel Weber, Frankfurt am Main

Vincenzo Desario, Rome

Antonio Fazio, Rome

David Dodge, Ottawa

Toshihiko Fukui, Tokyo

Timothy F Geithner, New York

Alan Greenspan, Washington

---

49   BIS, The BIS in profile, Bank for International Settlements flyer, June, 2005

Lord George, London

Hervï Hannoun, Paris

Christian Noyer, Paris

Lars Heikensten, Stockholm

Mervyn King, London

Guy Quaden, Brussels

Jean-Pierre Roth, Zürich

Alfons Vicomte Verplaetse, Brussels[50]

Of these, five members (Canada, Japan, the Netherlands, Sweden and Switzerland) are currently elected by the shareholders. The majority of directors are "ex officio," meaning they are permanent and are automatically a part of any sub-committee.

The combined board meets at least six times per year, in secret, and is briefed by BIS management on financial operations of the bank. Global monetary policy is discussed and set at these meetings.

It was reported in 1983 that there is an inner club of the half dozen central bankers who are more or less in the same monetary boat: Germany, U.S., Switzerland, Italy, Japan and England.[51] The existence of an inner club is neither surprising nor substantive: the whole BIS operation is 100% secret anyway. It is not likely that members of the inner club have significantly different beliefs or agendas apart from the BIS as a whole.

How the BIS works with the IMF and the World Bank

The interoperation between the three entities is understandably confusing to most people, so a little clarification will help.

The International Monetary Fund (IMF) interacts with governments whereas the BIS interacts only with other central banks. The IMF loans money to national governments, and often these countries are in some kind of fiscal or monetary crisis. Furthermore, the IMF raises money by receiving "quota" contributions from its 184 member countries. Even though the member countries may borrow money to make their quota contributions, it is, in reality,

---

50   BIS, Board of Directors, www.bis.org/about/board.htm.
51   Epstein, Ruling the World of Money, Harper's Magazine, 1983.

all tax-payer money.[52]

The World Bank also lends money and has 184 member countries. Within the World Bank are two separate entities, the International Bank for Reconstruction and Development (IBRD) and the International Development Association (IDA). The IBRD focuses on middle income and credit-worthy poor countries, while the IDA focuses on the poorest of nations. In funding itself, the World Bank borrows money by direct lending from banks and by floating bond issues, and then loans this money through IBRD and IDA to troubled countries.[53]

The BIS, as central bank to the other central banks, facilitates the movement of money. They are well-known for issuing "bridge loans" to central banks in countries where IMF or World Bank money is pledged but has not yet been delivered. These bridge loans are then repaid by the respective governments when they receive the funds that had been promised by the IMF or World Bank.[54]

The IMF is the BIS' "ace in the hole" when monetary crisis hits. The 1998 Brazil currency crisis was caused by that country's inability to pay inordinate accumulated interest on loans made over a protracted period of time. These loans were extended by banks like Citigroup, J.P. Morgan Chase and FleetBoston, and they stood to lose a huge amount of money.

The IMF, along with the World Bank and the U.S., bailed out Brazil with a $41.5 billion package that saved Brazil, its currency and, not incidentally, certain private banks.

Congressman Bernard Sanders (I-VT), ranking member of the International Monetary Policy and Trade Subcommittee, blew the whistle on this money laundry operation. Sander's entire congressional press release is worth reading:

IMF Bailout for Brazil is Windfall to Banks, Disaster for US Taxpayers Says Sanders

BURLINGTON, VERMONT - August 15 - Congressman Bernard Sanders (I-VT), the Ranking Member of the International Monetary Policy and Trade Subcommittee, today called for

52   IMF web site, http://www.imf.org.
53   World Bank web site..
54   Baker, op cit, p. 141-142

an immediate Congressional investigation of the recent $30 billion International Monetary Fund (IMF) bailout of Brazil.

Sanders, who is strongly opposed to the bailout and considers it corporate welfare, wants Congress to find out why U.S. taxpayers are being asked to provide billions of dollars to Brazil and how much of this money will be funneled to U.S. banks such as Citigroup, FleetBoston and J.P. Morgan Chase. These banks have about $25.6 billion in outstanding loans to Brazilian borrowers. U.S. taxpayers currently fund the IMF through a $37 billion line of credit.

Sanders said, "At a time when we have a $6 trillion national debt, a growing federal deficit, and an increasing number of unmet social needs for our veterans, seniors, and children, it is unacceptable that billions of U.S. taxpayer dollars are being sent to the IMF to bailout Brazil."

"This money is not going to significantly help the poor people of that country. The real winners in this situation are the large, profitable U.S. banks such as Citigroup that have made billions of dollars in risky investments in Brazil and now want to make sure their investments are repaid. This bailout represents an egregious form of corporate welfare that must be put to an end. Interestingly, these banks have made substantial campaign contributions to both political parties," the Congressman added.

Sanders noted that the neo-liberal policies of the IMF developed in the 1980's pushing countries towards unfettered free trade, privatization, and slashing social safety nets has been a disaster for Latin America and has contributed to increased global poverty throughout the world. At the same time that Latin America countries such as Brazil and Argentina followed these neo-liberal dictates imposed by the IMF, from 1980-2000, per capita income in Latin America grew at only one-tenth the rate of the previous two decades.

Sanders continued, "The policies of the IMF over the past 20 years advocating unfettered free trade, privatizing industry, deregulation and slashing government investments in health, education, and pensions has been a complete failure for low income and middle class families in the developing world and in the United States .Clearly, these policies have only helped corporations in their constant search for the cheapest labor and weakest environmental regulations. Congress must work on a new global policy that protects workers, increases living standards and improves the environment."

One can surmise that a financial circle exists where the World Bank helps nations get into debt, then when these countries can't pay their massive loans, the IMF bails them out with taxpayer money -- and in the middle stands the BIS, collecting fees as the money travels back and forth like the ocean tide, while assuring everyone that all is well.

BIS dumps gold-backed Swiss Francs for SDR's

On March 10, 2003, the BIS abandoned the Swiss gold franc as the bank's unit of account since 1930, and replaced it with the SDR.

SDR stands for Special Drawing Rights and is a unit of currency originally created by the IMF. According to Baker,

"The SDR is an international reserve asset, created by the IMF in 1969 to supplement the existing official reserves of member countries. SDR's are allocated to member countries in proportion to their IMF quotas. The SDR also serves as the unit of account of the IMF and some other international organizations. Its value is based on a basket of key international currencies."[55]

This "basket" currently consists of the euro, Japanese yen, pound sterling and the U.S. dollar.

The BIS abandonment of the 1930 gold Swiss franc removed all restraint from the creation of paper money in the world. In other words, gold backs no national currency, leaving the central banks a wide-open field to create money as they alone see fit. Remember, that almost all the central banks in the world are privately-held entities, with an exclusive franchise to arrange loans for their respective host countries.

---

55   IMF web site

Regional and Global Currencies: SDR's, Euros and Ameros

There is no doubt that the BIS is moving the world toward regional currencies and ultimately, a global currency. The global currency could well be an evolution of the SDR, and may explain why the BIS recently adopted the SDR as its primary reserve currency.

The Brandt Equation, 21st Century Blueprint for the New Global Economy notes, for instance, that

> Since the SDR is the world's only means of meeting international payments that has been authorized through international contract, **"The SDR therefore represents a clear first step towards a stable and permanent international currency"**[56] [bold emphasis added]

As to regional currencies, the BIS has already been hugely successful in launching the euro in Europe. Armed with new technical and social know-how, the BIS' next logical step is to focus on America and Asia.

For instance, according to BIS Papers No. 17, Regional currency areas and the use of foreign currencies,

> "Canada, Mexico and the United States are members of the trade group NAFTA. Given the high proportion of Canada and Mexico's trade with the United States, a NAFTA dollar or Amero has been proposed by some Canadian academics such as Grubel" (1999). See also Beine and Coulombe (2002) and Robson and Laidler (2002)."[57]

Assuming that NAFTA permanently identifies Canada, the U.S. and Mexico as one trading block, then North America will look like the European Union and the Amero will function like the Euro. All of the work put into the SDR would be perfectly preserved by simply substituting the Amero for the U.S. dollar when they choose to bring the Amero to ascendancy over the dollar.

For those American readers who do not grasp the significance

---

56   The Brandt Equation: 21 st Century Blueprint for the New Global Economy. The Brandt Proposals A Report Card: Money and Finances.
57   BIS, Regional currency areas and the use of foreign currencies, BIS Papers No. 17, September, 2003.

of the adoption of the euro by European Union countries, con-sider how one American globalist describes it.

C. Fred Bergsten is a prominent and core Trilateral Commission member and head of the Institute for International Economics. On January 3, 1999, Bergsten wrote in the Washington Post:

> *"The adoption of a common currency is by far the boldest chapter of European integration.* **Money traditionally has been an integral element of national sovereignty ...and the decision by Germany and France to give up their mark and franc ...represents the most dramatic volun-tary surrender of sovereignty in recorded history.** *The European Central Bank that will manage the euro is a truly supranational institution".[58] [bold emphasis added]*

Bergsten will have to rephrase this when the U.S. gives up the dollar for the amero -- that will become the most dramatic volun-tary surrender of sovereignty in recorded history!

Conclusions

Our credo is "Follow the money, follow the power." This chap-ter has endeavored to follow the money. We find that:

- The BIS is central bank to all major central banks in the world
- It is privately owned by central banks themselves, most of whom are also private
- It was founded under questionable circumstances by questionable people
- It is accountable to no one, especially government bodies
- It operates in complete secrecy and is inviolable
- Movement of money is obscured and hidden when routed through the BIS
- The BIS is targeting regional currency blocks and ulti-mately, a global currency
- It has been hugely successful at building the New International Economic Order, along with its attendant initiatives on global governance.

---

58   Washington Post, The Euro Could Be Good for Trans-Atlantic Relations, C. Fred Bergsten, January 3, 1999

EPILOGUE

NEW DEVELOPMENTS

The global monetary system is still functioning but closer to collapse than ever before, proving that there are limits to everything. The rise of populism and attacks on the so-called 'Deep State" should not be mistaken for any kind of permanent victory over the money-handlers of the world. The troika of global banking and their predecessors have been dominant for well over one hundred years, and have produced untold wealth for the cartels that supported them. Will they willingly walk away? Hardly.

The most significant monetary development in the last ten years has been blockchain and digital currencies like Bitcoin. This has been hailed by critics of globalization as a departure from control over money. Some say that it will completely dethrone the old-school bankers. However, the Bank For International Settlements is already staking its claim on this new technology:

> *DLT may radically change how assets are maintained and stored, obligations are discharged, contracts are enforced, and risks are managed. Proponents of the technology highlight its ability to transform financial services and markets by: (i) reducing complexity; (ii) improving end-to-end processing speed and thus availability of assets and funds; (iii) decreasing the need for reconciliation across multiple record-keeping infrastructures; (iv) increasing transparency and immutability in transaction record keeping; (v) improving network resilience through distributed data management; and (vi) reducing operational and financial risks. DLT may also enhance market transparency if information contained on the ledger is shared broadly with participants, authorities*

and other stakeholders.[35]

The current head of the IMF, Christine Lagarde, weighed in on March 14, 2018 by stating,

The same innovations that power crypto-assets can help us regulate them," she writes. Purpose-built distributed ledger systems could help regulators, governments, and markets share information more easily, she says. Combined with other technologies, like biometrics and AI, this approach could "help us remove the pollution from the crypto-assets ecosystem.[36]

The World Bank is also developing a strategy for cryptocurrency:

The adoption of cryptocurrency—a digital currency that employs cryptography to ensure that transactions are secure— as a mode of payment for a project allows the identification of each user of the money, unlike with traditional modes of payment like notes and coins. Though most popular cryptocurrencies, like bitcoin, are anonymous and only use a key to identify a user, **it is possible to include personal information, like the ID number, and make the cryptocurrency non-anonymous.** *The use of cryptocurrency also allows for instantaneous transactions and borderless transfer-of-ownership ("money with wings"), which reduces transaction time and cost, since financial intermediaries are not needed.[37]*
[emphasis added]

With such fanfare, it should not surprise the reader that the central banks are taking their lead from the Bank for International Settlements. The prestigious Stratfor reports:

In fact, several central banks, including the Bank of England and the U.S. Federal Reserve, have begun research into whether to issue digital currencies. Sweden's central bank, the Riksbank, has led the way in efforts to launch a digital

35   Bank for International Payments, "Distributed ledger technology in payment, clearing and settlement", 2017, p. 1.
36   MIT Technology Review, "The head of the IMF wants to turn blockchain technology against itself", Mike Orcutt, March 14, 2018.
37   WorldBank.org, "Can cryptocurrencies and blockchain help fight corruption?", Enrique Aldax-Carroll, February 20, 1018.

currency, the e-krona, and the governments of many other countries are eager to expedite the introduction of their own cryptocurrencies.[38]

The move toward cryptocurrencies is complimented by a carefully orchestrated global war on cash, thanks to all of the above-named organizations. This initiative intends to take all cash out of circulation, forcing all members of society to have a digital money account as well as a unique and universal identifier. The perpetrators complain about money laundering, drug running and other illegal activities while blaming cash itself. In the fine print it is noted that it really is a policy of "inclusion" where there will be "no person left behind."

No person left behind, indeed. At least two billion people in the world do not currently have a bank account, nor do they want one. These holdouts use cash for all of their financial transactions and value the anonymity that it provides. As cash is removed, they will be literally forced into the digital age whether protesting or not.

For the first time in history, the world is poised for a unified global monetary system that includes every person. Were it not for blockchain technology and cryptocurrencies like Bitcoin, none of this would be possible.

---

38   Worldview.Stratfor.com web site, "Why Central Banks Could Mint Their Own Digital Currency", March 28, 2018.